First in a series of Granny Goosefoot adventure books.

© 2021 Helen C. Ayers, All Rights reserved.
No part of this book may be reproduced, stored in a retrieval system or transmitted by any means without the written permission of the author.

Printed in the United States of America

ISBN: 978-1-7366760-5-9

Granny Goes To The Cruise

Written by Helen C. Ayers

As we all know Granny Goose loves to go on new adventures. Today she has decided to go on a boat ride on the nearby ocean where there are several excursion boats sitting at the dock, ready for those wishing to ride in one.

Granny quickly neatens her little straw-filled bed in her little goose house on Farmer Brown's farm so that when she returns from her boat ride, it will be ready for her to jump back into her little bed and rest. She, as always, leaves a large egg on her little pillow for Farmer Brown's wife to find because she likes to use them in her baking chores every day.

After she is ready to go, Granny clamps her little red hat that she loves so much onto her little head and hangs her little purse which contains her fare for the cruise ship and some food around her neck and then she is ready to go.

As she skips out of her little house, she sees her farm friends, the cow, the horse and the pig.

From long habit Granny asks each one of her friends if they would like to go for a cruise with her and as usual the cow says "Moo," and continues to chew on her cud; "Neigh," says the horse, "don't go there"; and "Oink" says the pig, "Bring me back something good to eat."

Seeing that Farmer Brown and his wife were not present, Granny quickly scooted under the broken fence where she began most of her adventures and headed down toward the ocean to get on the excursion boat.

Granny had just enough money in her little purse to pay her fees for the ride and to buy a little bit of something to eat and she was anxious to see what pleasure riding on a big ship could bring her.

Granny was assigned to ride on an upper deck which pleased her very much. From way up there she could see far, far away across the water and could see what the other people were doing down on a lower deck.

Some people on this excursion were eating lovely food and drinking some type of beverage she did not recognize but thought it looked very good. Others were dancing to music that was being played nearby; some were exercising and others were swimming in a pool of water!!!

This pool was something she had not expected to see. After all there was an ocean full of water all around them, yet there were many people in their little bathing suits swimming in a pool built on a deck below her. She decided she would join those in the pool after she had eaten her lunch.

At lunchtime Granny Goose ate a little bit of nearly everything on the buffet and drank some of the fruity-tasting drink everyone else seemed to be enjoying.

At first, Granny thought this was a wonderful idea. Then Granny realized that the motion of the water in the ocean and the water in the pool was moving at different rates and she began to feel very sick to her stomach. Too late, Granny remembered what overeating and drinking strange drinks had done to her when she went to the fair near her home.

The people around her began to look at her with a question on their faces.

Granny heard one of them say to the other, "I wonder if that old Goose is going to be sick to her stomach, I saw her eating an awful lot of food and drinking the wine."

Granny, not being used to the motions made by boats, and never having drunk any wine, soon realized she was going to be very sick to her stomach and jumped out of the pool and ran to the side of the boat to lean over the safety rail and began giving the ocean all the food she had eaten and drunk that day.

Below the water she could see huge fish swimming around and wondered if swimming made them sick to their stomachs. I bet it does, she thought to herself, as she finally stopped being sick over the rail.

One of the big fish swimming around in the ocean was a shark that had been following the path of the boat waiting for its own dinner. The shark would take whatever food was discarded from the kitchens, or better yet that plump goose who was staring at it over the side of the boat would do nicely.

"What a treat that fat goose would be," the fish thought.

Not long after that the ship made a wide turn and started back to shore for which Granny was glad.

Riding in a big boat like this one was just too much for her and she certainly would be much better off in her little straw bed on Farmer Brown's farm.

As soon as the ship had been tied up at the pier, Granny quickly left the boat and ran toward the hole in the fence through which she had made her escape from Farmer Brown and his wife.

As she passed her friends on the way to her little goose house, the cow said "Moo,"; the horse said "Neigh," and the pig said "Oink."

"Oh, don't ask me," Granny said, "I'm still very sick to my stomach."

Granny entered her little house and jumped into her little straw bed.

The egg was gone, her house was still neat and she was very tired. What a relief to be home, Granny thought. I don't think I will ever leave this little house and this farm again.

But we, and all her friends in the barnyard knew, that Granny would soon be off on another exciting adventure.

Made in the USA
Monee, IL
12 April 2022